CANCER:

A COMPLETE GUIDE TO THE CANCER ASTROLOGY STAR SIGN

Sofia Visconti

Contents

INTRODUCTION

Astrology has fascinated humans for centuries. At its core, it is the study of how celestial bodies like the Sun, Moon, planets and stars influence lives and natural events on planet Earth. It takes into account these entities' positions, at someone's birth time to create their natal or birth chart. This chart acts as a snapshot representing an individual's life path personality traits, strengths and challenges.

In this book we embark on a captivating exploration of astrology with a focus on the Cancer zodiac sign. Inside we aim to demystify astrology and provide you with an understanding of the Cancer zodiac sign. Cancer, represented by the crab, holds a key position in the zodiac. People born under this sign are recognized for their emotions, intuition and strong bonds with their homes and loved ones. By exploring the traits and characteristics of individuals with Cancer you will gain insights into your own life as well as those around you. Equipped with this knowledge you can navigate life's trials with enhanced clarity and purpose. Come join us on a journey as we unravel the mysteries of Cancer. A sign that encompasses both the moon's tranquil tides and a crabs protective shell.

CANCER ZODIAC SIGN OVERVIEW

- **Date of Star Sign**: Cancer falls between June 21st and July 22nd, making it the fourth sign of the zodiac in Western astrology.
- **Symbol**; The symbol of Cancer is the Crab. This choice of symbol reflects the nature of Cancer individuals. They often exhibit a protective, resilient and sometimes retreating exterior. Much like a crab's hard shell.
- **Element**; Cancer is associated with the Water element. Water signs are known for their deep emotional capacity and strong intuition.
- **Planet**; The ruling celestial body of Cancer is the Moon. Just as the Moon waxes and wanes, Cancer individuals are known for their fluctuating emotions.

- **Color**; Silver, white and pale shades of blue are often linked to this sign. These colors reflect the connection Cancer has with the Moon and water.

PERSONALITY TRAITS

Cancer is a zodiac sign known for its intricate and diverse personality traits. Here are some essential qualities often associated with individuals born under Cancer.

- **Emotional Sensitivity**; Cancers possess an understanding of their emotions and those of others. They have an empathy towards others feelings.
- **Nurturing**; They have an inclination to care for and support others making them exceptional caregivers and loyal friends.
- **Intuitive**; Cancer individuals possess a strong intuition. Often they pick up on things that might go unnoticed by others. Their instincts are usually spot on.
- **Home and Family Oriented**; They hold their home life and family in high regard considering it as a priority. Building a harmonious, home environment is of great importance to them.
- **Protective**; Similar to the shell of a crab, Cancers fiercely guard their loved ones. They often display remarkable determination when it comes to defending them.

STRENGTHS

- Compassion and empathy.
- Loyalty and devotion to loved ones.
- Strong nurturing instincts.
- Intuitive and perceptive.
- Creative and imaginative.

WEAKNESSES

- Tendency to be moody and emotionally sensitive.
- Can be overly cautious and hesitant to take risks.
- Difficulty letting go of the past.
- May become withdrawn when hurt or feeling vulnerable.
- Prone to mood swings.

COMPATIBILITY

When it comes to compatibility Cancer tends to get along well with Water signs, like Scorpio and Pisces. The emotional, intuitive nature they share makes for excellent connections. Additionally Earth signs such as Taurus and Virgo appreciate Cancer's nurturing qualities. Overall this can also contribute to compatibility. It's worth noting that individual factors beyond zodiac signs can influence compatibility well.

To summarize Cancer is a zodiac sign that is known for its emotions, caring nature and intuitive abilities. Represented by the crab it symbolizes both protection and sensitivity. Understanding the characteristics, strengths and weaknesses of Cancer individuals can provide insights into their compassionate personalities.

As we embark on this voyage this book aims to delve deeper into the qualities, strengths and weaknesses exhibited by Cancer individuals. It serves as a companion for self discovery and personal growth enabling readers to navigate life's challenges, with clarity and purpose. As we progress through the chapters we will explore the qualities of Cancer, its compatibility with other astrological signs and the symbolism behind it. Through this exploration you will acquire a comprehension of the Cancer zodiac sign and how its energies can influence not only your own life but also the lives of those in your vicinity. Come along on this journey as we uncover the nature of Cancer and embrace its energies for a truly meaningful and enriching existence.

CHAPTER 1:
HISTORY AND MYTHOLOGY

Welcome to the captivating realm of "Cancer", in History and Mythology a chapter that uncovers the tapestry of stories, legends and ancient wisdom associated with this sign. In this exploration we will embark on a journey through time delving into the observations of the "Cancer" constellation, its representations across different cultures and the lasting impact of this sign in modern astrology.

From the ancient records of Mesopotamia that first documented "Cancer" to the mythological narratives that have shaped its symbolism. This chapter invites you to unravel the enigmatic nature of this celestial sign. We will also examine how it has evolved from its origins into a tool for understanding human emotions in modern astrology.

As we set off on this adventure, get ready to be captivated by tales from eras passed and be enlightened by the significance of "Cancer" in our present lives. Whether you have an interest in astrology or simply hold curiosity about the origins and meaning behind your zodiac sign. Rest assured this chapter promises an enthralling exploration of Cancer.

HISTORICAL ORIGINS OF THE CANCER CONSTELLATION

The constellation known as Cancer, has a history that dates back thousands of years. Different ancient civilizations from around the world documented this group of stars. Each infusing their unique interpretations and meanings into it.

ANCIENT MESOPOTAMIA

The earliest recorded mentions of the Cancer constellation can be traced back to Mesopotamia to the Babylonians. They referred to this grouping as "MUL.AL.LUL," which translates to "the Crayfish" or "the Crab." The Babylonians associated this constellation with the Moon and its cycles symbolizing its connection to tides.

ANCIENT EGYPT

In ancient Egyptian astronomy Cancer was often linked with a scarab beetle. The scarab held significance as a symbol of transformation and rebirth since it was believed to push the Sun across the sky. Much like how dung beetles roll balls of dung. This interpretation emphasizes the relationship between the Cancer constellation and the apparent movement of the Sun in our skies.

ANCIENT GREECE AND ROME

The ancient Greeks and Romans adopted the crab representation for Cancer from their predecessors.

According to mythology the constellation known as Cancer is associated with one of Hercules' great challenges, where he encountered a crab sent by the goddess Hera. This intense battle resulted in the crab being immortalized among the stars serving as a lasting tribute to Hercules' heroic feats.

HINDU MYTHOLOGY

In Hindu mythology the constellation known as Cancer holds significance through the story of Daksha. According to legends Daksha created a daughter named Sati who later became Lord Shiva's wife. After Satis self immolation her ashes were scattered in the ocean. In Hindu cosmology it is believed that Cancer represents this aspect.

These historical and mythological connections have resulted in interpretations of the Cancer constellation, across cultures. Whether perceived as a crab scarab beetle or part of a pattern, Cancer's presence in the night sky has sparked awe and has been a source of storytelling throughout human history.

HISTORICAL EVENTS

Throughout history, significant events have taken place during the time period known as the Cancer season, in astrology. While it's important to note that the influence of astrology on events is subjective and open to interpretation there are a few happenings during this timeframe that have captured the attention of astrologers.

- **American Independence**; On July 4th the United States celebrates its independence coinciding with the Cancer season. This momentous occasion is seen by some astrologers as a turning point in history symbolizing the nation's sense of identity and resilience—characteristics often associated with individuals born under the Cancer sign.

- **French Revolution**; The French Revolution, which commenced in the century witnessed significant developments occurring within the Cancer season. The revolution was marked by emotions, passionate ideals and radical transformation. Traits that can be linked to Cancer's emotional depth and transformative nature.

HISTORICAL FIGURES BORN UNDER THE CANCER SIGN

Several influential historical figures who were born under the Cancer sign have left a mark on our world. Here are a few remarkable individuals who exemplify the characteristics of the Cancer zodiac sign.

- **Nelson Mandela** (born on July 18 1918); As a president of South Africa and a prominent anti apartheid activist Mandela showcased the enduring spirit, emotional strength and unwavering commitment to justice. Such traits that are commonly associated with Cancer.

- **Napoleon Bonaparte** (born on July 15 1769); Known for his brilliance and reign. The emperor Napoleon embodied the ambitious nature, resolute determination and exceptional leadership qualities. Such traits are often attributed to those born under the Cancer sign.

EVOLUTION OVER TIME

The understanding and interpretation of the zodiac sign Cancer has undergone significant changes over time. In old times people associated this constellation and sign with tales and celestial symbolism. However as astrology has advanced in the modern era, interpretations have shifted towards a more psychological and personality based approach.

In ancient civilizations like Babylon and Greece, astrology was closely intertwined with religion and mythology. Astrologers primarily studied celestial patterns for their significance and guidance. As the centuries passed astrology underwent a transformation by incorporating advancements ultimately evolving into the astrology we are familiar with today.

Modern astrologers focus on an individual's personality traits and tendencies while exploring how the energies associated with this sign influence one's life, relationships and personal growth. The shift from interpretations to insights reflects a broader trend in astrologys evolution. One from being primarily mystical and predictive to becoming a tool for self exploration and personal growth.

In conclusion the zodiac sign known as Cancer holds an important place in the tapestry of human history. It has been intertwined with legends, cultural interpretations and celestial symbolism. From its early documented observations in Mesopotamia to its multifaceted representations across cultures, Cancer has significantly influenced our collective imagination.

As we have explored this constellation has transformed over time, transitioning from a mythological concept to an astrological tool. A tool that sheds light on psychological tendencies and personality traits. The enduring legacy of Cancer extends beyond its importance. As such it continues to provide insights into our emotions.

For those interested in delving further into the history and mythology surrounding Cancer here is a list of recommended resources for further reading;

FURTHER READING AND REFERENCES

- "The Secret Language of Astrology: The Illustrated Key to Unlocking the Secrets of the Stars" by Roy Gillett.
- "The Oxford Companion to Astrology" by Nicholas Campion.

- "Astrology: History, Symbols, and Signs" by R. A. Waldie.
- "Myths of the Zodiac: A Colorful Illustrated History of the Heavens" by Anna Southgate.
- "The Zodiac and the Salts of Salvation: Homeopathic Remedies for the Sign Types" by George W. Carey.
- "The Living Stars: An Account of the Fixed Stars in Astrology" by Dr. Eric Morse.

CHAPTER 2:
LOVE & COMPATIBILITY

Welcome to the captivating realm of "Cancer" Love and Compatibility. Join us on a journey, through the depths of emotions and harmonious unions experienced by individuals born under the Cancer zodiac sign. In the following pages we will explore the tendencies, desires and dynamics that shape Cancer individuals relationships. From their nurturing and empathetic nature to their search for security we will uncover factors that influence their approach to love and partnerships.

Furthermore this chapter explores how Cancer interacts with each of the other zodiac signs. Whether you are a Cancer or someone with one, we will unveil insights into the dynamics of love between Cancer and each sign. These insights can assist you in navigating the complexities of your relationships. Prepare yourself for a dive into emotions as we explore the bonds forged by Cancer individuals and gain an understanding of their intimate connections.

LOVE APPROACH

Cancer individuals approach love and romance with strong emotions, sensitivity and a desire for intimacy. Those born under the Cancer sign are known for their nurturing nature, which extends to their relationships. Let's take a closer look at how Cancer individuals approach love and romance.

- **Emotional Bond;** Cancer individuals place importance on emotional connection in their romantic relationships. They seek partners who can understand, appreciate and reciprocate their needs. Cancer individuals tend to express their feelings showing how much they care for their loved ones.

- **Nurturing**; Similar to how they're caring and protective within their families Cancer individuals extend this care to their partners as well. They have an inclination towards taking care of the needs of those they love. Maybe it involves simple acts of kindness such as cooking or being a good listener.

- **Focus on Home and Family**; Creating a harmonious home environment with their partners holds value for Cancer individuals. They often envision building a nest while sharing domestic responsibilities. The concept of home and family is deeply cherished by them.

- **Loyalty**; When it comes to loyalty and commitment, in relationships Cancer individuals excel. When they choose someone as their partner they tend to be deeply committed. They highly value long term relationships. As such they are willing to invest the time and effort to nurture them.

- **Empathy**; Cancer individuals possess a nature that allows them to be highly attuned to their partners emotions. They often have a sense of when something's wrong or when their partner needs support. Their empathetic qualities make them exceptional at providing comfort and understanding.

- **Stability**; In relationships Cancer individuals seek security and stability. They are naturally drawn to partners who can offer them safety and a sense of belonging. Financial stability and a solid foundation also hold importance for them.

- **Honesty and openness**; Although Cancer individuals may not always express their feelings verbally they tend to demonstrate their affection through actions and gestures. Open and honest communication is highly valued by them particularly when it comes to addressing concerns.

- **Vulnerability**; Cancer individuals embrace vulnerability within their relationships. They understand that true intimacy requires sharing fears, dreams and insecurities with a partner. This willingness to be authentic strengthens the bonds they develop.

- **Affection**; Romantic gestures and tokens of affection hold significance for Cancer individuals as they appreciate these expressions of love.

- **Experience**; Cancer individuals take pleasure in crafting experiences, for their significant others. Be it through arranging unexpected romantic outings or leaving heartfelt messages.

To summarize, Cancer's perspective on love and romance is characterized by emotions, caring, loyalty and a deep longing, for both security and closeness. They are devoted partners who prioritize the happiness and welfare of their loved ones.

COMPATIBILITY WITH OTHER ZODIAC SIGNS

Cancer is a water sign in astrology, and individuals born under this sign are known for their nurturing and emotional nature. When it comes to love and compatibility with other zodiac signs, Cancer's compatibility can vary depending on the partner's sign. Let's explore how Cancer interacts with each of the other twelve zodiac signs.

CANCER AND ARIES

Cancer and Aries have contrasting personalities. Cancer seeks emotional security and stability. On the other hand Aries is adventurous and impulsive. While there can be initial attraction due to their differences, long-term compatibility may be challenging due to their conflicting needs and communication styles.

CANCER AND TAURUS

Cancer and Taurus are both nurturing signs and share a deep appreciation for stability. They connect on an emotional level and create a loving partnership. These two signs can build a strong and lasting relationship based on mutual support and shared values.

CANCER AND GEMINI

Cancer and Gemini have different approaches to relationships. Cancer is emotional and values commitment. Gemini is more intellectually driven and enjoys variety. Their differences can lead to misunderstandings and challenges in maintaining a long-term connection. However, with effort and compromise, they can make it work.

CANCER AND CANCER

When two Cancer individuals come together, there is a deep understanding of each other's emotions. They share a strong emotional connection and can create a loving and supportive home life. However, they may also struggle with mood swings and emotional sensitivity. This can lead to occasional conflicts.

CANCER AND LEO

Cancer and Leo have contrasting personalities. Cancer is introverted and nurturing. Leo is outgoing and confident. They may initially be drawn to each other's differences. Although long-term compatibility can be challenging due to Leo's need for attention and Cancer's need for emotional security.

CANCER AND VIRGO

Cancer and Virgo can complement each other well. Virgo's practicality balances Cancer's emotional nature. Thus they can work together to create a stable and loving partnership. Their attention to detail and commitment to one another can make for a successful relationship.

CANCER AND LIBRA

Cancer and Libra have different needs in a relationship. Cancer desires emotional connection and security. Libra seeks balance and harmony. They may enjoy each other's company. However, they might struggle to fulfill each other's emotional needs, leading to potential challenges.

CANCER AND SCORPIO

Cancer and Scorpio share a deep emotional connection. They both value intensity and commitment in relationships, making them highly compatible. Their passionate and loyal natures can lead to a strong and lasting bond.

CANCER AND SAGITTARIUS

Cancer and Sagittarius have very different outlooks on life and relationships. Cancer seeks security and stability, while Sagittarius craves adventure and freedom. These differences can lead to misunderstandings and could make long-term compatibility challenging.

CANCER AND CAPRICORN

Cancer and Capricorn can create a harmonious partnership. Capricorn's stability and Cancer's emotional depth complement each other. They share a commitment to building a secure and nurturing home life, making for a strong foundation in their relationship.

CANCER AND AQUARIUS

Cancer and Aquarius have contrasting personalities and communication styles. Cancer is emotional and nurturing. Aquarius is intellectual and independent. These differences can lead to challenges in understanding each other's needs and perspectives.

CANCER AND PISCE

Cancer and Pisces are both water signs. This means they share a deep emotional connection. They understand each other's feelings intuitively and can create a loving and supportive relationship. Their compatibility is often characterized by empathy, romance, and shared dreams.

Remember that in astrology, while compatibility can provide insights into the dynamics of a relationship, it's essential to remember that individual personalities and experiences play a significant role in how two people connect and build a successful partnership. Remember people can overcome differences with effective communication, understanding and mutual respect.

TIPS FOR DATING AND MAINTAINING RELATIONSHIPS WITH CANCER INDIVIDUALS

IF YOU'RE DATING A CANCER WOMAN

- Give her time to open up and share her feelings at her pace. Be patient and understanding.
- Plan dates that create an atmosphere, like cooking dinner or having an intimate picnic in a peaceful location.

- Show genuine empathy and listen attentively when she talks about her emotions. Offer support when she needs to vent or express herself.
- Show interest in her family as they hold importance in her life.
- Be there for her emotionally, during times providing comfort and a shoulder to lean on.

IF YOU'RE DATING A CANCER MAN

- Help him create a home environment as Cancer men value their homes as havens.
- Be patient and reassuring during his moments of sensitivity or insecurity. Let him know your feelings and commitment are steadfast.
- Cancer men have an inclination towards caregiving. Show appreciation for the things he does to take care of you whether it's preparing a meal or offering an embrace.
- Cancer men often have artistic interests. Participate in activities that he enjoys and is passionate about.
- Loyalty holds importance for Cancer men. Show your commitment to the relationship. Assure him of your faithfulness.

GENERAL TIPS FOR DATING AND MAINTAINING RELATIONSHIPS WITH

INDIVIDUALS BORN UNDER THE SIGN OF CANCER

- **Respect their need for space**; While Cancer individuals are nurturing, they also value their time. Respect their desire for solitude. Avoid pressuring them to open up when they're not ready.
- **Share your emotions**; Cancer individuals appreciate openness. Be willing to share your feelings and concerns with them as it helps strengthen the bond.
- **Celebrate occasions**; Remember dates such as anniversaries or birthdays. Put thought into meaningful gifts or gestures.
- **Offer support**; Cancer individuals are likely to have dreams and aspirations. Be supportive of their goals and provide encouragement.
- **Establish trust**; Trust forms the foundation of any relationship. Be open and honest, in your communication to establish a foundation of trust.
- **Plan outings**; Cancer individuals enjoy settings. Arrange dinners at home stargazing sessions or peaceful walks in nature.
- **Show gratitude**; Express your appreciation for their care and support. Recognize the efforts they put into nurturing the relationship.

Remember that everyone is unique and these suggestions serve as guidelines. It's crucial to understand the preferences and needs of the Cancer individual you are dating and adapt your approach accordingly. Developing a nurturing and lasting bond requires patience, empathy and genuine affection.

Throughout this chapter we have delved into the realm of Cancer individuals exploring their characteristics, desires and their unique ways of approaching matters of the heart. As we conclude this chapter let us again remember that astrology offers insights into the complexities of relationships. Understand that each person is unique. In the end love is a voyage of exploration, personal development and forming connections. Love indeed resembles a constellation that illuminates our lives, leading us through its transforming and captivating patterns.

CHAPTER 3: FRIENDS AND FAMILY

Welcome to this chapter which delves into the dynamics of friendship and family relationships that define those born under the Cancer zodiac sign. Within these pages we will uncover the essence of Cancer, as friends and family members. Prepare to be moved by the warmth and depth found within Cancers friendships and family connections. If you happen to be a Cancer sign looking to embrace your traits or if you simply want to understand the Cancer individuals, in your life better this chapter guarantees an exploration. One filled with empathy, affection and the lasting connections that characterize the star sign Cancer.

CANCER AS A FRIEND

Being friends with a Cancer individual is like stumbling upon a treasure filled with unwavering support. People born under the Cancer zodiac sign are known for their ability to forge meaningful connections with their friends. They embody the essence of being a "ride or die" friend you can always rely on. Let's take a closer look at what it means to have a Cancer friend.

- **Emotional Support**; Cancer friends serve as your go to support system. They possess an intuition that allows them to sense when something is bothering you even without you having to say a word. Be it celebrating your achievements or when going through tough times they are always there to offer their comforting presence.

- **Nurturing**; Like the crab, their symbol. Cancer friends have an inherent nurturing instinct. They take pleasure in taking care of their friends whether it's by preparing home cooked meals, giving thoughtful gifts or simply checking in on you.

- **Loyalty**; When it comes to loyalty Cancer friends stand unmatched. They remain steadfastly by your side through thick and thin. Their loyalty is unwavering, making them friends you can rely on.

- **Events**; They enjoy planning events such as movie nights celebrating friendship anniversaries and ensuring that every holiday goes well.

- **Like family**; Cancer friends often consider their friends as part of their family. They warmly welcome you into their homes creating a sense of belonging and comfort that's hard to find.

- **Intuitive**; Cancer friends possess strong intuition. They have an ability to perceive your moods and feelings, even when you try to conceal them. This intuitive understanding enables them to provide the kind of support when you need it the most.

- **Patience and forgiveness**; these are virtues cherished by Cancer friends. They know everyone has their own imperfections and they readily overlook them. In case of any misunderstandings they are quick to extend a branch and mend the friendship.

- **Resolution**; Conflict resolution is a priority, for Cancer individuals who prefer peace, within friendships. If conflicts arise they will diligently work towards finding resolutions that preserve the bond between friends. They place a value on their friendships and strive to make sure they endure over time.

- **Empathy and Compassion**; Friends who are Cancer zodiac sign individuals possess a sense of empathy and compassion. They genuinely care about your well being. As such they will go the extra mile to ensure your happiness.

Ultimately when you have a Cancer friend you will discover a companion who nurtures your spirit, supports your aspirations and treasures your friendship. While they may have their shell once you are granted access you will encounter the warmth and unwavering dedication that characterizes Cancer as a friend.

FAMILY DYNAMICS

The Cancer astrological sign represents a connection to family, home and deep emotional bonds. People born under this sign are profoundly influenced by their family dynamics. They are well known for their attachment to their loved ones. Let's explore how Cancer individuals interact within the context of their families.

- **Nurturing**; Those with the Cancer sign naturally take on the role of nurturers within their families. They ensure that everyone is well taken care of, both physically and emotionally.

- **Emotional Pillars**; Cancer individuals serve as support systems within their families. They become the go to person when someone needs a listening ear or advice. Their empathetic nature allows them to connect with family members on a deep level.

- **Home Focused**; Cancer is synonymous with home. Those born under this sign often prioritize creating an inviting environment in their homes. They take pride in their living spaces and place importance on preserving family traditions while also establishing ones.

- **Loyalty**; Loyalty holds value, for Cancer individuals. They wholeheartedly devote themselves to their families. As such they typically go above and beyond to protect and support them. Through thick and thin they remain steadfast by the side of those they love.

- **Family Dynamics and Sensitivity**; People born under the Cancer zodiac sign are highly attuned to the dynamics within their families. They possess an ability to detect tension or underlying emotions. In turn they actively work towards resolving conflicts and restoring harmony.

- **Preserving Traditions**; Cancer individuals place value on tradition and often take on the role of preserving family customs, rituals and celebrations. They ensure that these cherished traditions are passed down from one generation to the next.

- **Addressing Conflict with Care;** Despite their preference for harmony Cancer individuals are not afraid to address family conflicts. With tact and sensitivity they navigate these situations in order to find resolutions.

- **Encouraging Independence**; While deeply connected to their families Cancer individuals also understand the importance of fostering individuality and independence among family members. They encourage their loved ones to pursue their dreams while providing unwavering support along the way.

In conclusion it is evident that cancer's influence on family dynamics is profound.

They are like the backbone of their families offering encouragement, nurturing affection and devotion. Despite their somewhat cold exteriors Cancer individuals willingly expose their feelings and demonstrate an unwavering dedication, towards fostering a loving household.

CHALLENGES IN FRIENDSHIPS AND FAMILY RELATIONS

While people born under the zodiac sign of Cancer are often recognized for their positive impact they also encounter challenges in their relationships with friends and family. Understanding these challenges can assist both Cancer individuals and their loved ones in navigating their relationships. Here are some common obstacles they may face.

- **Emotional Sensitivity**; Cancer individuals possess a sensitivity to the emotions of others which can sometimes become overwhelming for them. They may absorb emotions from family members or friends resulting in strain and exhaustion.

- **Overprotective**; The protective instincts of Cancer individuals can occasionally manifest as overprotectiveness. They may feel compelled to shield their loved ones from difficulty. Ultimately this can lead to feelings of suffocation.

- **Letting Go**; People belonging to the Cancer sign often find it challenging to let go of hurts or conflicts. They may hold onto grudges or dwell on wounds for a long period of time, placing strain on their relationships.

- **Fear of Rejection**; Due to their heightened sensitivity Cancer individuals may experience a fear of rejection or abandonment. This fear can make them hesitant to open up to friends or initiate conversations about topics within their families.

- **Mood Swings**; Cancers, governed by the Moon are known for their mood swings. Navigating through their fluctuations can be challenging for loved ones who may not always comprehend the root cause of these changes.
- **Traditional Values**; Cancer individuals place importance on tradition and family customs. However their strong attachment to these traditions can sometimes make it difficult for them to embrace change or adapt.
- **Emotional Boundaries;** Cancer individuals occasionally face difficulties in establishing boundaries. They often prioritize others' needs above their own which can result in fatigue over time.

Remember that dealing with these challenges, in friendships and family relationships requires communication, patience and understanding from both parties involved. People with Cancer zodiac signs can benefit from learning how to express their emotions and finding ways to handle their sensitivity. Friends and family members can contribute to the success of these relationships by respecting boundaries, offering support and openly addressing any issues in a caring manner.

As we wrap up this chapter lets take a moment to consider how we can enhance, sustain and cultivate these connections, with Cancer individuals;

IMPROVING RELATIONSHIPS

- **Foster Open Communication**; Encourage Cancer individuals to honestly express their feelings. This promotes better understanding.
- **Respect Personal Boundaries**; Recognize and honor their need for time and personal space. Strive for a balance between closeness. Respect boundaries.
- **Conflict Resolution**; Handle conflicts with sensitivity and empathy when they arise. Cancer individuals dislike confrontation. Approach discussions calmly with a focus on finding solutions.

MAINTAINING STRONG RELATIONSHIPS

- **Express Appreciation**; Regularly show gratitude for their nurturing and supportive nature. Small acts of appreciation can make a difference in maintaining a bond.

- **Embrace Traditions;** Participate in family traditions and rituals. These hold meaning for Cancer individuals as they strengthen family ties.
- **Support Them Emotionally;** Be there for them in tough times, just like they are for you. Offer support, lend a listening ear and provide comfort whenever needed.

BUILDING STRONGER RELATIONSHIPS

- **Shared Activities;** Take part together in activities that strengthen the bond between you. Whether it's cooking together, sharing stories or attending family gatherings. Together these experiences can deepen your connection.
- **Create Meaningful Memories;** Put effort into making memories and traditions together. Cancer individuals greatly appreciate such moments. Value the efforts put into building new ones.
- **Encourage Independence;** Support Cancer individuals in pursuing their interests and hobbies. Assure them of your backing. Striking a balance between individuality and togetherness fosters growth. Ultimately it leads to healthier relationships.

In essence nurturing and developing relationships with Cancer individuals requires patience, understanding and embracing their qualities. By fostering communication, respecting boundaries and offering support you can create lasting bonds that reflect Cancers nurturing and loving nature. As you embark on this journey of connection and love, with your Cancer friends and family members may your hearts forever be touched by the warmth and depth of these enduring relationships.

CHAPTER 4:
CAREER AND AMBITIONS

Welcome to this chapter dedicated to exploring the relationship between individuals born under the Cancer zodiac sign and their professional lives. Within these pages we aim to uncover the qualities, strengths and challenges that Cancer individuals bring to their careers and financial endeavors. Furthermore we will look into their approach to financial matters.

Throughout this chapter we'll provide strategies for achieving success in the workplace while offering insights into money management. Whether you are a Cancer seeking guidance in your career and financial pursuits. Or if you're someone eager to gain a better understanding of Cancer individuals, rest assured this chapter holds valuable insights.

CANCER CAREER PREFERENCES AND PROFESSIONAL ASPIRATIONS

Individuals, with the Cancer zodiac sign possess a set of qualities and strengths that can greatly benefit their lives. They are driven by their depth, empathy and strong sense of responsibility. This often leads them to find fulfillment in careers where they can make an impact on others. Now let's take a closer look at the career preferences and professional aspirations of those born under the zodiac, Cancer.

- **Nurturing**; Caring for others comes naturally to Cancer individuals making them excel in professions related to healthcare, nursing, counseling, social work and psychology. Their innate empathy and ability to connect with people on a deep level make them exceptional caregivers.
- **Home body**; Due to their attachment to home and family, Cancer individuals often gravitate towards careers that revolve around these themes. They may find fulfillment as stay at home parents. As such they often pursue professions such as designing, real estate or work related to home renovation.

- **Emotionally Intelligent**; With their emotional intelligence, Cancer individuals thrive in careers that require understanding and managing emotions. They shine in roles such as human resources management, conflict resolution specialists or coaching positions where they can assist individuals in navigating their feelings and relationships.

- **Leaders**; Teaching and education naturally align with the interests of Cancer individuals. They derive joy from nurturing minds and guiding students through their journeys. As such they might choose to pursue careers in education. For example, as teachers, professors or counselors.

- **Foodies**; Cancer individuals often find joy in creating a home atmosphere that extends to their love for cooking. Many of them thrive as chefs, bakers or food stylists deriving pleasure from preparing meals and curating a dining experience.

- **Attention to detail**; Entrepreneurship is an area where Cancer individuals excel due to their skills and meticulous attention to detail. Their dedication and unwavering commitment contribute significantly to the triumph of their business ventures.

- **Security;** Cancer individuals are sometimes drawn towards careers in finance because they place a priority on security. They demonstrate proficiency in roles that involve planning and analysis such as financial advisors or investment analysts.

- **Philanthropy**; Driven by a desire to make an impact on society, Cancer individuals often find fulfillment in professions relating to philanthropy. They naturally enjoy charity initiatives and philanthropic endeavors where they can contribute meaningfully towards causes they care about.

- **Creativity**; With their creative inclinations Cancer individuals may explore paths within creative professions such as writing, music or the arts. These outlets enable them to express themselves while tapping into their inner world.
- **Management and Leadership**; Cancer individuals have the potential to excel as managers and leaders in positions that foster a nurturing atmosphere.

To summarize Cancer individuals' career preferences and professional aspirations are deeply influenced by their caring nature, emotional intelligence and desire to establish a comfortable environment. They thrive in roles that allow them to care for others, make an impact and contribute to the well being of their colleagues or clients.

STRENGTHS THAT MAKE CANCER INDIVIDUALS EXCEL IN THE WORKPLACE:

Individuals, with the zodiac sign Cancer, bring a distinguished set of strengths to the workplace. Of course this makes them valuable assets in professional environments. Their innate ability to nurture and empathize, coupled with their emotional intelligence greatly contribute to their success. Here are some notable strengths that distinguish Cancer individuals in the workplace.

- **Empathy and Compassion**; People born under the sign of Cancer possess a large capacity for empathy and compassion. This allows them to deeply understand the emotions and needs of their colleagues and clients. Overall this leads to fostering relationships and teamwork.
- **Strong Emotional Intelligence**; Cancer individuals exhibit a high level of emotional intelligence enabling them to navigate complex dynamics within the workplace with finesse.
- **Loyalty and Dedication**; Known for their loyalty and dedication Cancer individuals take their commitments seriously. They are willing to go above and beyond to achieve their goals and support their teams.
- **Excellent Team Players;** Cancer individuals thrive in team settings as they possess a team nature that promotes collaboration among team members. Often taking on the role of an anchor within the team they foster unity among colleagues while boosting morale and productivity.
- **Problem Solvers**; When it comes to problem solving, those born under Cancer approach it with creativity and sensitivity in mind. They consider both aspects well, as emotional nuances when seeking innovative solutions that address diverse needs.
- **Organizational Skills**; Their ability to pay attention to detail and stay organized is truly

impressive. Cancer individuals shine in roles that involve planning and effectively managing resources, projects or teams.

- **Adaptability**; While they appreciate stability Cancer individuals are also adept, at adapting to circumstances and embracing challenges. Their flexible nature allows them to thrive in dynamic work environments.

- **Dependability**; Colleagues and supervisors often rely on Cancer individuals because of their dependability. They are trusted team members who prioritize meeting deadlines and fulfilling their responsibilities.

- **Strong Work Ethic**; Cancer individuals possess a work and approach their professional duties with utmost seriousness. They are known for their diligence, thoroughness and persistent efforts in achieving their goals.

- **Intuition**; Their intuitive instincts serve as an asset when it comes to decision making. Cancer individuals often have a sense about situations or people which helps them make informed choices.

- **Attention to Well Being**; Prioritizing the well being of both themselves and their colleagues is paramount, for Cancer individuals. They actively promote self care and stress reduction. Maintaining a work life balance is important for them to create a happier and more productive workplace environment.

- **Leadership Potential**; With their nurturing and supportive leadership style Cancer individuals naturally excel as leaders. They inspire trust,

loyalty while also serving as mentors and role
models.

To summarize individuals born under the Cancer
zodiac sign, possess valuable qualities in terms of empathy,
emotional intelligence, loyalty and a strong work ethic.
They thrive in positions that involve fostering connections,

with others promoting teamwork and creating a harmonious atmosphere.

CAREER CHALLENGES AND STRATEGIES TO OVERCOME THEM

While individuals born under the zodiac sign of Cancer bring strengths to the workplace they also face challenges that can impact their professional development. Understanding these challenges and implementing strategies to overcome them can help Cancer individuals thrive in their careers. Let's explore some challenges and corresponding strategies.

Sensitivity to Feedback

- Challenge; Cancer individuals may take criticism personally leading to hurt feelings and a dip in confidence.
- Strategy; Focus on feedback rather than perceiving it as a personal attack. Seek guidance from mentors to gain a perspective on your performance and grow through feedback.

Difficulty Establishing Boundaries

- Challenge; Cancer individuals often struggle with setting boundaries. This can result in taking on much and experiencing burnout.
- Strategy; Practice assertiveness. Learn to say no when necessary. Prioritize self care. Establish limits to avoid overextending yourself.

Fear of Change

- Challenge; Cancer individuals tend to prefer stability and may be resistant to change making it challenging for them to adapt in paced industries.
- Strategy; Embrace change as an opportunity for growth. Stay updated with industry trends. Proactively seek ways to expand your skills ensuring you remain competitive.

Emotional Overwhelm

- Challenge; The emotional demands of the workplace can sometimes overwhelm Cancer individuals impacting their productivity.
- Strategy; Take steps towards managing emotions by seeking outlets outside of work such as meditation or hobbies that provide rejuvenation.

Avoiding conflict

- Challenge; Cancer individuals have a tendency to avoid conflict. This can result in issues in the workplace.
- Strategy; It is important to learn conflict resolution skills and practice clear communication. By addressing conflicts you can prevent them from escalating and find productive resolutions.

Indecisiveness

- Challenge; Cancer individuals can be indecisive when it comes to career choices. This often stems from their desire for security and fear of making the wrong decision.

- Strategy; Seeking guidance from mentors or career counselors can help clarify your career goals. Breaking down decisions into manageable steps can make the process less overwhelming.

Blurred boundaries

- Challenge; Cancer individuals tend to identify with their careers making it difficult for them to separate work from their lives.
- Strategy; Establishing boundaries between work and personal life is crucial. Engaging in activities outside of work that bring joy and fulfillment can help maintain a work life balance.

Procrastination

- Challenge; Procrastination is another obstacle that Cancer individuals commonly face. It often leads to missed deadlines.
- Strategy; Setting goals and prioritizing tasks can help overcome procrastination tendencies. Breaking projects into smaller steps not only reduces overwhelm but also ensures timely completion.

In conclusion we have explored the connection between Cancer individuals and their professional lives as well as their distinct approach to money. Throughout this chapter we have uncovered the strengths, challenges and strategies that define how a Cancer pursues success.

Individuals belonging to the Cancer zodiac sign bring a wealth of intelligence and dedication to their careers due to their nurturing and nature. Their unwavering loyalty, resilience and commitment to creating work environments make them highly valuable in a range of professions. Moreover their focus on home and family extends to their aspirations as they strive to provide security and stability for their loved ones.

However, like individuals from any zodiac sign Cancers also face certain challenges. These challenges include sensitivity towards criticism and a reluctance when it comes to self promotion. Nevertheless these obstacles can be seen as opportunities for growth and development. By embracing change, setting boundaries, improving communication skills and developing conflict resolution abilities; Cancer individuals can overcome these hurdles and achieve their career objectives.

As we wrap up this chapter it's important to remember that the path to success and financial well being is different for everyone. Whether you're a Cancer sign aiming to thrive in your career and finances or someone intrigued by the approach to work and money let the insights we've shared here serve as guidance on your journey towards a prosperous life. Like the phases of the moon your professional growth and financial circumstances may fluctuate. But with patience, determination and the wisdom of the Crab you'll be able to navigate life's ups and downs, with grace and resilience.

CHAPTER 5: SELF-IMPROVEMENT

Welcome to a new chapter where we embark on a journey of growth and development! A journey specifically for those born under the Cancer zodiac sign. Their journey towards self improvement is deeply rooted in their desire to enhance their lives while providing unwavering support to their loved ones. Within these pages we uncover how Cancer individuals can harness their strengths, overcome weaknesses and navigate the path to personal growth.

From embracing change and setting boundaries to nurturing well being and fostering resilience. This chapter offers insights and strategies for Cancer individuals to embark on a journey of self discovery and improvement. Whether you are seeking to enhance your life or someone interested in understanding the unique path of personal growth for Cancer individuals this chapter promises valuable guidance.

PERSONAL GROWTH AND DEVELOPMENT

Personal growth and development deeply resonates with Cancer individuals. Nurtured by their compassionate nature, they have a drive to become the best versions of themselves. Now let's explore some key aspects of growth and development for Cancer individuals.

- **Introspection**; Reflecting on oneself and being aware of emotions. Cancer individuals can greatly benefit from self reflection and emotional awareness. Taking time to understand their feelings and motivations helps them navigate life with clarity and purpose. Practices, like keeping a journal or practicing meditation can support this process.
- **Establishing boundaries;** Cancer individuals often find it challenging to set boundaries since they naturally prioritize taking care of others. However, learning to set and maintain boundaries is crucial for their growth ensuring they balance their own needs with their nurturing instincts.
- **Developing conflict resolution skills**; As individuals who dislike conflict Cancer individuals can enhance their development by acquiring

conflict resolution skills. This empowers them to address issues in a manner while maintaining harmony in their relationships.

- **Embracing change**; Cancer individuals tend to prefer stability over change. However personal growth often requires stepping out of one's comfort zone. Learning to embrace change as an opportunity for growth becomes an aspect of their development journey.

- **Practicing self care and stress management**; Considering their inclination, towards caring for others individuals born under the zodiac sign Cancer might sometimes overlook the importance of self care. It becomes crucial for them to prioritize self care routines. Relaxation techniques and strategies to manage stress are a good idea.

- **Communication skills**; Improving communication skills especially when it comes to expressing their needs and desires can empower Cancer individuals in their journey of growth. Effective communication plays an important role in fostering understanding and establishing connections with others.

- **Goal setting**; Setting attainable goals is beneficial for Cancer individuals. Whether these goals pertain to their career, relationships or personal aspirations. Overall having a roadmap helps them stay focused and motivated on their path of growth.

- **Resilience**; Developing resilience is a part of growth for Cancer individuals. Life inevitably presents challenges along the way. However, nurturing resilience allows them to bounce back stronger than before.

- **Independence**; Cultivating independence is an area where Cancer individuals can focus on as they tend to prioritize others needs over their own. Learning how to stand on one's feet and pursue interests contributes significantly to one's growth and self discovery.
- **Creativity**; Cancer individuals possess creative potential. Exploring outlets such as art, writing or music can provide a fulfilling avenue for them to express themselves artistically and emotionally.
- **Learning**; The love for learning and innate curiosity are deeply ingrained within Cancer individuals. They have an inclination towards learning that serves as a catalyst for continuous personal growth.
- **Seek support;** In the case of Cancer individuals, they should not hesitate in seeking support when needed. Just as they offer support to others. Whether it's through therapy, counseling or mentorship, seeking guidance can greatly contribute to growth.

To summarize, personal growth and development, for Cancer individuals involves deepening awareness, establishing and maintaining boundaries embracing change and fostering resilience. By prioritizing self care, communication and nurturing their creativity Cancer individuals can aspire to become resilient and authentic individuals as they continue to evolve. Lastly, remember that personal development is an individual journey where individuals have the opportunity to continuously expand their knowledge and skills throughout their lives.

HARNESSING STRENGTHS AND OVERCOMING WEAKNESSES:

Those born under Cancer's zodiac possess a unique blend of strengths and weaknesses that shape their character. By embracing their strengths and working on areas for improvement they can embark on a journey of growth and self improvement. Here's a look at how they can achieve that.

Empathy and Compassion (Strength)

- Embrace; Utilize your empathy to foster meaningful connections. Provide support to loved ones. Consider pursuing careers where you can make a positive difference in others lives.
- Overcome; Be mindful not to shoulder the burdens of others. Practice establishing boundaries to prevent burnout.

Strong Emotional Intelligence (Strength)

- Embrace; Utilize your intelligence to navigate social situations effectively. Employ it to build rapport, resolve conflicts and excel in roles that require understanding and managing emotions.
- Overcome; Avoid overanalyzing situations. Avoid being overly sensitive to criticism. Recognize that not everything carries a weight.

Loyalty and Dedication (Strength)

- Embrace; Channel your loyalty and dedication towards achieving your career goals. Commit to your projects, team members and personal endeavors. Your determination can pave the way for long term success.
- Overcome; Exercise caution, in remaining in situations that no longer contribute positively to you.

Security focus Strength)

- Embrace; Embrace your cautious approach. Build a secure future for yourself and your loved ones. Develop budgeting and savings habits. Consider long term investment opportunities for financial stability.
- Overcome; Avoid worrying too much about security. Strike a balance between saving for the future and enjoying the present.

Handling Criticism Sensitively (Weakness)

- Embrace; Transform your sensitivity towards criticism into an opportunity for growth. Use feedback as a tool to enhance your skills and improve yourself.
- Overcome; Develop resilience by focusing on self confidence and self worth. Remember that not all criticism reflects your abilities.

Reluctance to Promote Yourself (Weakness)

- Embrace; Recognize the importance of self promotion in your career. Highlight your accomplishments and skills when appropriate and take credit for your contributions.
- Overcome; Practice self affirmation and build confidence in yourself. Acknowledge your achievements. Remind yourself of your value.

Fear of Change (Weakness)

- Embrace; Embrace change as a chance, for growth and new experiences. Understand that change can lead to both professional development.
- Overcome; Developing adaptability involves taking steps of your comfort zone. Gradually exposing yourself to experiences can help you build confidence, in navigating through changes.

Remember that by capitalizing on your strengths and actively addressing any weaknesses, individuals with the Cancer zodiac sign can embark on a fulfilling journey of self improvement. This balanced approach allows them to continue nurturing and supporting others while also nurturing their own development.

Throughout this chapter we have delved into their strengths, weaknesses and the strategies they can employ to become the versions of themselves. As Cancer individuals embrace growth and development they can look forward to better relationships, increased self assurance and the ability to navigate life's ever changing circumstances, with confidence. Ultimately each step you take brings you closer, to becoming the best version of yourself.

CHAPTER 6: THE YEAR AHEAD

In this chapter we offer individuals born under the Cancer zodiac sign a glimpse into the upcoming year. As celestial bodies align, their influence will shape your life in many ways. This chapter serves as your guiding compass through the events that may impact the many aspects of your life. As we traverse through these events and their implications Cancer individuals will gain valuable insights. These insights will help you to navigate challenges, seize opportunities and make the most of this year. So my dear friend, let's embark on this voyage guided by the stars as we embrace all the possibilities that await us.

HOROSCOPE GUIDE FOR THE YEAR AHEAD

As you begin a journey, around the sun the vast universe has a tale to share with you. Here is your horoscope guide for the year ahead providing insights into the energies that will impact your life.

Aries season (March 21. April 19)

- Relationships; Make harmony a priority in your relationships. Be open to compromise and understanding as this will strengthen the connections you share.
- Career; New opportunities might come your way. Trust your instincts. Embrace challenges to progress in your path.

Taurus season (April 20. May 20)

- Finances; Keep an eye on your financial situation. Budget wisely. Consider long term investments for future stability.
- Health; Prioritize your well being through a healthy lifestyle. Eat clean. Take up regular physical activity.

Gemini season (May 21. June 20)

- Career; Your professional life is poised for growth. Embrace new roles and projects as they will lead you towards advancement.
- Travel; Explore the idea of travel or engaging in pursuits to broaden your horizons and gain fresh perspectives.

Cancer season (June 21. July 22)

- Self Discovery; Focus on growth and self exploration. Be receptive to change and establish boundaries that nurture your well being.
- Family; Strengthen ties, through communication and quality time spent together.

Leo season (July 23. August 22)

- Creativity; Your creative energy will shine as you explore creative pursuits or hobbies that ignite your passion.
- Love; Love and romance may flourish during this time. Cherish these moments. Nurture your relationships.

Virgo season (August 23. September 22)

- Career; You have the potential for career advancements within your reach. Your meticulous approach and dedication will lead to success.
- Health; Take care of yourself by prioritizing a diet and regular exercise.

Libra season (September 23. October 22)

- Love; Foster harmony in your relationships through quality communication and if necessary compromise.
- Money; Ensure stability through long term planning and responsible spending.

Scorpio season (October 23. November 21)

- Self improvement; Embark on a journey of self discovery and personal growth. Explore your potential to evolve as an individual.
- Travel; Consider expanding your horizons through travel or educational opportunities.

Sagittarius season (November 22. December 21)

- Career; Pursue your career ambitions with fresh enthusiasm as new opportunities and challenges will lead to advancement.
- Family; Strengthen family bonds. Create a nurturing home environment.

Capricorn season (December 22. January 19)

- Money; Focus on achieving stability through budgeting and wise long term investments.
- Health; Make sure to take care of both your mental and physical health by finding a balance in your life.

Aquarius season (January 20. February 18)

- Friendships; It's important to nurture your friendships and expand your circle. Collaborative opportunities might lead to lucrative ventures.
- Romance; Be open to new possibilities. Embrace the connections.

Pisces season (February 19. March 20)

- Self Care; Remember to prioritize self care and relaxation. Taking time for rest and rejuvenation is crucial for your overall well being.
- Career; There's potential for career growth. Trust your intuition when making career related decisions.

So as you embark on the journey of the year remember that while the cosmos can offer guidance it is ultimately your choices and actions that will shape your destiny. Embrace the opportunities that come your way, learn from challenges and trust in your wisdom. May this year bring you growth, love and fulfillment in many ways.

KEY ASTROLOGICAL EVENTS

Astrological events play an important role in shaping the experiences and energies that impact individuals born under the Cancer zodiac sign. Here are some important astrological events and how they can potentially affect Cancer individuals.

New Moon in Cancer

- Impact; The New Moon in Cancer brings a surge of fresh energy making it an ideal time for setting intentions related to growth, family matters and emotional healing.
- How it affects Cancer; During this time Cancer individuals may experience heightened intuition and emotional depth. It's an opportunity for self care and nurturing relationships.

Full Moon in Capricorn

- Impact; The Full Moon in Capricorn often highlights career and ambition. It will be shedding light on areas where balancing work and home life is necessary.
- How it affects Cancer; Cancer individuals may find themselves managing dual responsibilities between their personal lives. Remember it's important to maintain harmony while prioritizing self care.

Jupiter Transits

- Impact; When Jupiter, the planet of expansion and growth enters or aligns favorably with the sign of Cancer it can bring many opportunities. Notably for personal development, travel and education.

- How it affects Cancer; During these times Cancer individuals may feel a desire for learning new things and exploring new horizons. Now is the perfect time to expand your knowledge and focus on personal development.

Saturn Transits

- Effects; When Saturn transits it can bring challenges and lessons related to responsibilities. For Cancer individuals it may be an opportunity to evaluate their commitments and make some adjustments.
- How it impacts Cancer; Cancer individuals might feel inclined to bring better organization and discipline into their lives. Although these transits can be demanding they offer chances for growth and maturity.

Mercury Retrograde

- Effects; During Mercury Retrograde there may be disruptions in communication and technology. It's a period for reflection and reevaluation.
- How it impacts Cancer; Cancer individuals should be cautious of miscommunications and delays during this time. Utilize this period for introspection and revisiting decisions.

Eclipses

- Effects; Solar and lunar eclipses have the potential to bring changes in both professional and personal aspects of life. They often signify a shift in focus or the beginning of a new chapter in life.
- How it impacts Cancer; Eclipses can inspire Cancer individuals to reassess their goals, relationships and overall life direction. Embrace these changes as opportunities for growth.

Venus Transits

- Effects; Venus transits highlight matters of love, relationships and beauty. They can create opportunities for romance, as enhanced creativity.
- How Cancer is influenced; They may experience a boost in harmonious energies during Venus transits. It's a period for nurturing relationships and expressing their creativity.

These astrological events bring a backdrop to the lives of Cancer individuals. By understanding the effects of these events they can make better informed choices, embrace opportunities for personal growth and navigate challenges.

Below are some key areas to consider in the year ahead.

LOVE AND RELATIONSHIPS

In the realm of love and relationships, Cancer individuals are deeply influenced by the celestial movements of the year. Let's delve into how astrological events will impact their romantic lives.

New Moon in Cancer

- Impact: The New Moon in Cancer is an emotional powerhouse. It sets the stage for self-discovery and renewed commitment in relationships.
- Advice: Embrace this time to strengthen your emotional bonds with loved ones. Reflect on your desires and communicate openly with your partner.

Venus in Cancer

- Impact: Venus, the planet of love and beauty, graces Cancer with its presence. This period may bring increased romance and sensuality.
- Advice: Nurture your romantic relationships during Venus' stay in your sign. Plan special dates and express your affection openly.

Mars Retrograde

- Impact: Mars Retrograde can create tension and conflicts in relationships. Misunderstandings may arise, leading to introspection.
- Advice: Be patient and avoid unnecessary confrontations. Use this time to reflect on your desires and consider the long-term health of your relationships.

Solar and Lunar Eclipses

- Impact: Eclipses can bring pivotal changes in love and relationships. They may signify new beginnings or the end of certain connections.
- Advice: Embrace change and transformation. Be open to the opportunities that eclipses bring, even if they initially seem challenging.

CAREER AND FINANCES

Astrological events also play a significant role in shaping Cancer individuals' career and financial prospects. Here's how the celestial movements of the year ahead may impact these areas.

Jupiter in Pisces

- Impact: Jupiter's influence in Pisces may bring career growth and expansion. Financial opportunities could well be on the horizon.
- Advice: Seize professional opportunities with enthusiasm. Invest in your skills and knowledge to maximize your career potential.

Saturn in Aquarius

- Impact: Saturn's presence in Aquarius may prompt career reassessment. It encourages a focus on long-term goals and financial stability.
- Advice: Take a disciplined approach to your career and finances. Build a solid foundation for your future and consider necessary changes.

Mercury Retrograde

- Impact: Mercury Retrograde can lead to miscommunications and delays in financial matters. Caution is advised in money-related decisions.
- Advice: Double-check contracts and financial agreements. Use this time for careful financial planning and budgeting.

HEALTH AND WELLNESS

Cancer individuals' well-being is closely tied to key astrological events. Let's explore how these cosmic movements may affect their health and offer guidance for maintaining wellness.

Solar and Lunar Eclipses

- Impact: Eclipses can trigger stress and emotional challenges, potentially affecting physical health.
- Advice: Prioritize self-care during eclipse periods. Maintain a balanced routine, practice relaxation techniques, and seek support when needed.

Venus in Leo

- Impact: Venus in Leo brings a boost of vitality and self-confidence. It's an excellent time for self-care and enhancing overall well-being.
- Advice: Focus on self-care routines that make you feel confident and radiant. Engage in physical activities that bring you joy.

PERSONAL GROWTH AND SELF-DISCOVERY

Astrological events offer opportunities for personal growth and self-discovery. Here's how Cancer individuals can make the most of the year ahead.

New Moon in Cancer

- Impact: The New Moon in Cancer invites self-reflection and the setting of new intentions.
- Advice: Use this time for deep self-discovery. Set intentions for personal growth and emotional healing. Embrace change with an open heart.

Saturn in Aquarius

- Impact: Saturn's presence in Aquarius encourages self-examination and personal growth.
- Advice: Embrace the challenges as opportunities for growth. Focus on long-term goals and cultivate resilience.

Solar and Lunar Eclipses

- Impact: Eclipses mark moments of transformation and new beginnings.

- Advice: Embrace change with an open mind. Use eclipses as catalysts for positive personal growth and self-discovery.

Overall in the year ahead, Cancer individuals can harness the energy of these astrological events to nurture their relationships, advance their careers, enhance their well-being and embark on a journey of self-discovery. By staying attuned to the cosmic currents, they can ultimately navigate the challenges ahead. At the same time they can seize the opportunities that arise.

The vast expanse of the cosmos with its dance of movements and celestial alignments reveals valuable insights into what lies ahead in the coming year. As we say goodbye to this chapter remember that while astrology gives us guidance it's up to you to shape your destiny. Move forward with bravery and determination! May the upcoming year be like a canvas. One where you can create a picture filled with love, success, health and personal growth.

CHAPTER 7:
FAMOUS "CANCER" PERSONALITIES

In this chapter we will embark on a journey through the lives of people who were born under the Cancer zodiac sign. As we delve into the stories of these figures from fields such as entertainment, politics, sports and business we will uncover the distinct qualities that have propelled them towards greatness. Join us as we celebrate their achievements. Let us also navigate through their challenges and explore how these famous Cancer individuals have made an impact. Whether you share a Cancer sign or simply seek inspiration from their journeys this chapter promises to be an exploration. One that explores how stars have influenced some of history's most influential figures.

HENRY VIII

- Date of Birth: June 28, 1491.
- Brief Biography: Henry VIII was the King of England from 1509 to 1547. He is best known for his six marriages and his role in the English Reformation.
- Cancer Traits: Henry displayed traits of sensitivity, loyalty, and a deep emotional nature often associated with Cancer individuals.

- Impact: His reign was marked by significant political and religious changes, including the establishment of the Church of England.
- Personal Life: His marital struggles and quest for a male heir are legendary, leading to his separation from the Catholic Church.

DIANA SPENCER (PRINCESS DIANA)

- Date of Birth: July 1, 1961.
- Brief Biography: Princess Diana was the first wife of Prince Charles and a beloved member of the British royal family. She was known for her philanthropy and humanitarian work.
- Cancer Traits: Diana embodied the nurturing and empathetic qualities of Cancer individuals, making her a compassionate figure.
- Impact: Her charitable endeavors and efforts to destigmatize issues like HIV/AIDS had a lasting impact on global awareness.
- Personal Life: Diana's personal life, including her public struggles and divorce from Prince Charles, garnered significant media attention.

JOHN D. ROCKEFELLER

- Date of Birth: July 8, 1839.
- Brief Biography: John D. Rockefeller was an American business magnate and philanthropist who co-founded the Standard Oil Company.
- Cancer Traits: His strong sense of financial security and dedication to family align with Cancer's traits.

- Impact: Rockefeller's business empire revolutionized the oil industry and made him one of the wealthiest individuals in history.
- Personal Life: His philanthropic endeavors, including the creation of the Rockefeller Foundation, have had a lasting impact on education and public health.

ARIANA GRANDE

- Date of Birth: June 26, 1993.
- Brief Biography: Ariana Grande is a renowned American singer, songwriter, and actress known for her powerful vocal range.
- Cancer Traits: She embodies Cancer's emotional depth and artistic creativity, often infusing her music with personal experiences.
- Impact: Grande's music career has achieved immense success, earning numerous awards and a dedicated fan base.
- Personal Life: She's known for her resilience in the face of personal challenges, including the Manchester Arena bombing during her concert.

LIONEL MESSI

- Date of Birth: June 24, 1987.
- Brief Biography: Lionel Messi is an Argentine professional footballer often regarded as one of the greatest soccer players in history.
- Cancer Traits: Messi exhibits Cancer's dedication, emotional intelligence, and strong work ethic on the field.

- Impact: His exceptional skills have earned him numerous accolades, including multiple FIFA Ballon d'Or awards.
- Personal Life: Messi's commitment to philanthropy is reflected in his work with children's charities and UNICEF.

MIKE TYSON

- Date of Birth: June 30, 1966.
- Brief Biography: Mike Tyson is a former professional boxer known for his ferocious fighting style and being the youngest heavyweight champion.
- Cancer Traits: Despite his tough exterior, Tyson has spoken about his emotional nature, a characteristic of many Cancer individuals.
- Impact: He left a significant mark on the boxing world with his dominance and intense fighting style.
- Personal Life: Tyson's tumultuous personal life and legal issues have been well-documented.

ELON MUSK

- Date of Birth: June 28, 1971.
- Brief Biography: Elon Musk is a tech entrepreneur and CEO known for founding companies like SpaceX and Tesla.
- Cancer Traits: Musk's determination, visionary thinking, and occasional emotional intensity align with Cancer characteristics.

- Impact: His ventures are at the forefront of space exploration and electric vehicles, pushing technological boundaries.
- Personal Life: Musk's public persona often includes candid expressions of his thoughts and feelings on social media.

LIV TYLER

- Date of Birth: July 1, 1977.
- Brief Biography: Liv Tyler is an American actress known for her roles in films like "The Lord of the Rings" trilogy.
- Cancer Traits: Her gentle and empathetic on-screen presence reflects the qualities of Cancer individuals.

- Impact: Tyler's acting career has spanned various genres, earning her acclaim in both film and television.
- Personal Life: She's known for her close-knit family and artistic endeavors.

MALALA YOUSAFZAI

- Date of Birth: July 12, 1997.
- Brief Biography: Malala Yousafzai is a Pakistani education activist and Nobel Prize laureate who advocates for girls' education.
- Cancer Traits: Her unwavering determination, compassion, and commitment to education align with Cancer traits.
- Impact: Malala's advocacy has led to global recognition and support for girls' education worldwide.
- Personal Life: She continues to inspire and promote change through her work.

50 CENT (CURTIS JACKSON)

- Date of Birth: July 6, 1975.
- Brief Biography: 50 Cent is a renowned American rapper, actor, and producer known for his influence on hip-hop.
- Cancer Traits: His emotional depth and determination align with Cancer characteristics, influencing his music and career.

- Impact: 50 Cent has made a significant impact on the music industry and ventured into various business endeavors.
- Personal Life: He has faced personal and legal challenges but continues to thrive in his career.

BENAZIR BHUTTO

- Date of Birth: June 21, 1953.
- Brief Biography: Benazir Bhutto was the first woman to lead a Muslim-majority country, serving as Pakistan's Prime Minister.
- Cancer Traits: Bhutto exhibited Cancer's strong leadership qualities, nurturing spirit, and emotional intelligence.
- Impact: Her political career had a transformative impact on Pakistan's history, emphasizing democracy and women's rights.
- Personal Life: Bhutto's political journey was marked by challenges, including periods of exile and political opposition.

SELENA GOMEZ

- Date of Birth: July 22, 1992.
- Brief Biography: Selena Gomez is an American singer, actress, and producer known for her versatile talents.
- Cancer Traits: She reflects Cancer's emotional depth in her music and her commitment to mental health advocacy.

- Impact: Gomez has achieved fame as both a musician and actress, using her platform to raise awareness about important issues.
- Personal Life: She has been open about her struggles with mental health, contributing to reducing stigma.

As we contemplate the stories of these legends we are reminded that while cosmic alignment at birth plays a role it is only part of the equation. Their unwavering resolve and dedication to their callings have propelled them towards greatness.

Whether you find inspiration in their journeys, relate to their shared characteristics or simply value their contributions. Overall the lives of these Cancer individuals provide us with a glimpse into the diverse tapestry of human existence. They serve as a reminder that while celestial bodies above may guide our paths it's ultimately our efforts, resilience and dedication that truly shape our destinies.

CONCLUSION

As we approach the end of this eye opening journey into the realm of Cancer, the Zodiac Sign it's time to pause and reflect on the array of knowledge we have gathered together. Throughout this book we have delved deeply into the world of Cancer. We have unraveled its essence and its profound impact on individuals' lives. Let us now revisit the main points that have shed light on our understanding of Cancer.

Individuals born under this sign are characterized by their depth, empathy and nurturing nature. Their remarkable intuition and strong connection to family and home define them. The symbol associated with Cancer, the Crab represents their shell and their ability to navigate through a sea of emotions. Being a water sign emphasizes how emotions and intuition hold importance in their lives. The Moon governs Cancer symbolizing change and emotional cycles. Furthermore it amplifies their connection to emotions while reflecting their evolving nature.

People born under the sign of Cancer are well known for their loyalty, sensitivity and commitment. They thrive in roles that require empathy and compassion making them natural caregivers. Their strong intuition, nurturing nature and adaptability are what make them truly shine. They have a knack for creating holistic environments not just for themselves but also for those around them. Though sometimes Cancers can be overly emotional, sensitive to criticism and experience mood swings. Learning to balance their emotions can be an ongoing journey throughout their lives.

In our exploration throughout this book we have delved into the origins of Cancer, its significance in mythologies as well as its evolution within astrology over time. We have witnessed how Cancer has influenced events and notable figures while also playing a role in personality based astrology. From matters of love and relationships to friendships, family dynamics and career aspirations – we have extensively covered the aspects that shape the lives of individuals born under the sign of Cancer. Alongside providing tips and guidance on navigating challenges we have offered insights on nurturing strengths and pursuing growth. Let's now summarize the chapters we have traversed.

- **Chapter 1: History and Mythology**; In Chapter 1, we delved into the historical origins of the Cancer constellation and explored how different cultures perceived and represented it in their star maps. We also journeyed through the rich tapestry of "Cancer" in ancient mythologies, uncovering the stories and symbolism associated with this zodiac sign.
- **Chapter 2: Love & Compatibility**; Chapter 2 illuminated the intricacies of love and relationships for Cancer individuals. We examined their approach to romance and compatibility with other zodiac signs. The chapter also provided valuable tips for dating and maintaining relationships with Cancer partners.

- **Chapter 3: Friends And Family**; Chapter 3 delved into the dynamics of friendships and family relations for Cancer individuals. We explored their nurturing nature and the challenges they may encounter. In addition we looked at how to improve, maintain and grow these essential connections.

- **Chapter 4: Career And Money**; In Chapter 4, we uncovered Cancer individuals' career preferences and professional aspirations. We also discussed their strengths and challenges in the workplace. Inside we provided strategies to overcome obstacles and thrive in their chosen fields.

- **Chapter 5: Self-Improvement**; Chapter 5 offered insights into personal growth and development for Cancer individuals. We explored how they can harness their strengths and overcome weaknesses. Overall it facilitates self-improvement and achieving their potential.

- **Chapter 6: The Year Ahead**; Chapter 6 provided a horoscope guide for Cancer individuals in the year ahead. The chapter provided analysis of astrological events and their influence on their lives. Overall it offered valuable advice on making the most of the year ahead.

- **Chapter 7: Famous "Cancer" Personalities**; In Chapter 7, we celebrated the achievements of famous Cancer personalities. We explored the lives and legacies of individuals born under this zodiac sign. From political leaders to artists, athletes, and business moguls. These profiles illustrated how Cancer traits shaped their journeys to greatness.

Throughout the chapters of this book we have embarked on an exploration of the Cancer zodiac sign. From its ancient origins, to its relevance in aspects of life today we have gained comprehensive insights and a deeper understanding. Whether you're a Cancer individual seeking self discovery or simply intrigued by this sign. You have truly been on a rich and enlightening journey through the world of Cancer.

This book serves as a reminder that astrology, rooted in wisdom yet relevant today, continues to offer guidance on understanding our personalities and navigating our life paths. As we reach the end of this book lets carry with us the knowledge we've gained about Cancer and all the zodiac signs. May it empower us to have a better understanding of ourselves, our loved ones and the world around us. The stars above continue to guide us and through astrologys wisdom we embark on a journey of discovering ourselves and growing as individuals.

Thank you for joining us on this adventure through the realm of Cancer. May the cosmic energies always light up your path towards fulfillment, understanding and harmony with the universe. We committed to unraveling the enigmas surrounding the Cancer zodiac sign. By exploring aspects of life through a Cancer lens we have fulfilled this commitment. Ultimately this book serves as a guide for individuals born under Cancer assisting them in embracing their qualities while navigating lifes ups and downs. Above all else, our goal is for readers to understand that astrology, including the Cancer zodiac sign, provides a framework for self discovery and personal growth. Embracing our qualities, strengths and weaknesses is essential, for leading an harmonious life.

To conclude, astrology serves as a timeless language that resonates with individuals seeking insights into themselves and their life paths. The Cancer zodiac sign offers a perspective on the world characterized by depth nurturing qualities and resilience. For all those who identify as Cancer individuals we encourage you to embrace your qualities with pride. Your intuition, empathy and dedication are your strengths that will guide you towards a life filled with creativity and meaningful connections.

Astrology beckons us to connect with the cosmos and gain a deep understanding of ourselves and the world around us. Like all signs of the zodiac Cancer is a tapestry of potentials waiting to be woven into a fulfilling life. Continue your journey of self discovery while allowing the stars above to illuminate your path. Embrace who you truly are and cultivate your strengths. Allow the guidance of the stars to illuminate a bright pathway to follow. A pathway towards a brighter and more harmonious future.

Best wishes to you